Soft Shells

Sophia Vyzoviti,
Soft Shells: Porous and Deployable Architectural Screens
www.sophiavyzoviti.com

BIS Publishers
Building Het Sieraad
Postjesweg 1
1057 DT Amsterdam
The Netherlands
T (31) 020 515 02 30
F (31) 020 515 02 39
bis@bispublishers.nl
www.bispublishers.nl

ISBN 978-90-6369-269-8

Copyright © 2011 Sophia Vyzoviti and BIS Publishers

Graphic Design: Pieterjan Grandry & Valentina Karga
www.pieterjangrandry.com
www.valentinakarga.com

Printed in China

Sophia Vyzoviti

Soft Shells

Porous and Deployable Architectural Screens

BISPUBLISHERS

Contents

Sophia Vyzoviti

Introduction

'Soft Shells: Porous and Deployable Architectural Screens' comprises an anthology of form generation experiments which employ the continuous surface, its aggregates, and its subdivisions as a tool. Conducted primarily in analogue media, in a low-tech, high-concept fashion, experiments confront the geometry of surface transformations with material effects, incorporating factors such as gravity, time, and human participation. Research has been developed in the academic studio – in courses and workshops – as well as within professional practice. Applications of the morphogenetic experiments presented include exhibition installations, interior design, architectural models, and detailing prototypes. Four processes of surface transformations organise research findings, thus structuring the chapters of this book: 'cut', 'pleat', 'tile' and 'weave'. They operate on two conceptual levels. As techniques, they are associated with the craft of textiles. As vehicles of architectural thinking, they evoke the textile as a retro-novel paradigm for architectural design. According to Gottfried Semper, the textile precedes, informs, and later becomes consolidated into architecture. In the first volume of 'Style in the Technical and Tectonic Arts; Or, Practical Aesthetics', the textile is exemplified as the earliest artistic technique, comprising in essence "a system of material units whose attributes are pliability, suppleness, and toughness" whose basic objectives are "to string and to bind" as well as "to cover, to protect, to enclose". Within this framework, surface transformations, aggregates and subdivisions are investigated as a pre-tectonic (or proto-tectonic) condition where structural and ornamental characteristics of architecture may originate.

The material outcomes of the research presented are simultaneously abstract and concrete. They can be considered as architectural prerequisites and as proto-tectonic constructs. This methodological shift allows speculations on a novel constitution of the architectural object addressing aspects of the current architectural debate interwoven around the notions of surface, ornament, patterns, parametricism, and the performative. Emulating its origination in the animate textile, a soft and malleable, light and flexible, kinetic architectonic entity emerges. This entity primarily performs articulated within events producing plastic - and static - three-dimensional forms as side affects. The prototypical surfaces included in the anthology, intricate in form and formation, acquire an elementary enclosing and en-clothing capacity. They share properties of porosity and deployability, conditions that render them absorbent and spongy, transformable and multitasking, allowing them to become interfaces that support permeability and infiltration, mediating between environmental and social dipoles, in this sense comprising soft shells.

'Soft Shells' can be considered as a follow-up to my previous publications, 'Folding Architecture' and 'Supersurfaces'. Research continues in the lineage of surface transformations and employs design knowledge developed in the past. While the former investigated 'folding' as a material diagram in architectural design and the latter explored applications in a fusion design field between architecture, product design, and fashion, 'Soft Shells' investigates notions of the textile as a retro-novel architectural paradigm. This is evident in research goals and methods. The textile is employed as a relativistic device which encompasses both surface and ornament, generates patterns, and alludes to the performative as a responsive system. In this sense, the softness of architectural shells resides not only in their material substance - which is certainly flexible, malleable, and elastic - but also in their transient establishments, their inscriptions in performances and short-term architectural applications, as well as their weak or unstable forms. Furthermore, softness relates to their morphogenetic processes which oscillate in the dipole between artefact and representation, intuitive and computational, analogue and digital, individual and collective. These form generation processes accentuate malleability and flexibility. In compliance, the 'unfold' emerges as a novel architectural representation: a drawing of the animated three-dimensional surface returning to flat state and baring the traces of its transformations, cuts, pleats, and creases.

'Soft Shells' is essentially a visual narrative. Three essays are juxtaposed – or intertwined – engaging in a loosely structured dialogue with the work presented. 'Articulating Collapsible Universes' by Olga Toulumi provides a historical milestone for deployable structures, as a tribute to Buckminster Fuller. 'Surface Fatigue' by Igor Siddiqui explores the new status of surface as a multitasking striated entity within the discourse on digital materiality. 'Participatory Form-finding' by Sophia Vyzoviti addresses process-driven design methodologies that stimulate the creation of a creative community through the culture of making. The essays embed the relevance of the research to state-of-the-art architectural discourse, adding a certain historical, conceptual, and operational depth to the form-generating surface.

cut.

pleat.

1.1 acrylic

1.2 synthetic leather

1.3 polyethelene

1.4 opaline paper

2.1 nylon

2.2 corrugated cardboard

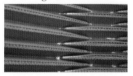

2.3 corrugated cardboard & ductape

2.4 cotton & cardboard

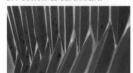

2.5 cardboard

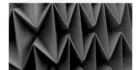

tile. weave.

3.1 terracotta

3.2 opaline paper

3.3 polypropelene
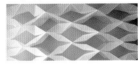

3.4 opaline paper

3.5 opaline paper in paraffin

3.6 foam rubber

4.1 opaline paper

4.1.1 cardboard

4.1.2 paperboard

4.1.3 opaline paper
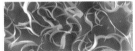

4.1.4 aluminum

4.1.5 cancon paper

4.2 corrugated cardboard

cut.

pleat.

1.1

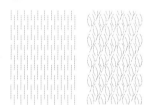

2.1

1.2

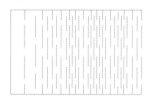

2.2

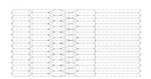

1.3

2.3

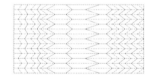

2.4

1.4

2.5

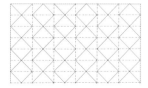

tile.

weave.

3.1

3.2

3.3

3.4

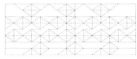

3.5

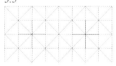

3.6

4.1

4.1.1

4.1.2

4.1.3

4.1.4

4.1.5

4.2

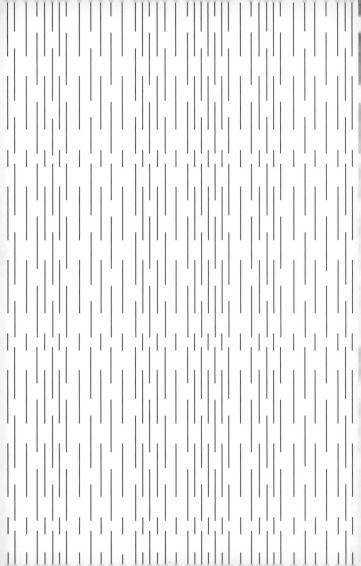

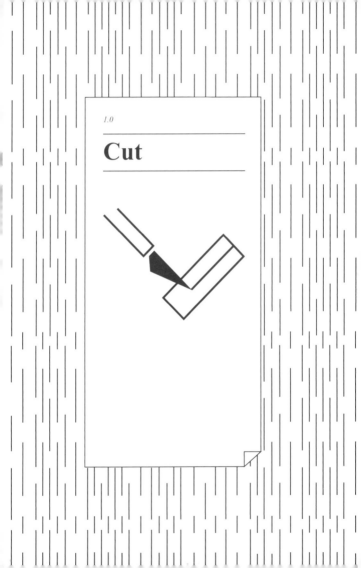

1.0

Cut

cut - stretch

The series of objects manifests augmentation and curvature of a single surface as it performs under tension. In material terms, the experiment utilises the elastic behaviour of a perforated sheet of acrylic along the horizon of its thermal malleability, in the ten seconds before it settles into a plastic form. Local variability of the overall regular pattern that striates it emerges in this interval. Patterns tested here include line segments and arcs in alternating rows, as well as randomly distributed splines.

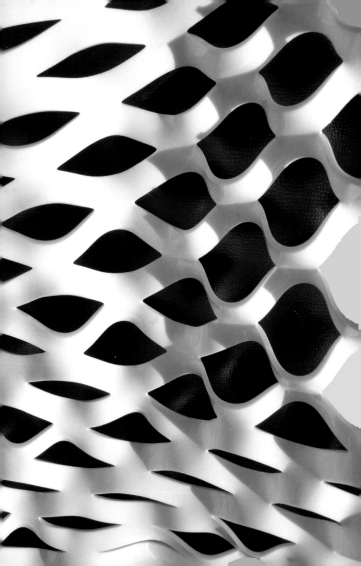

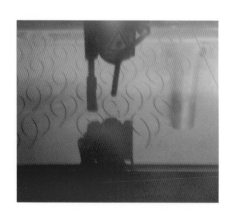

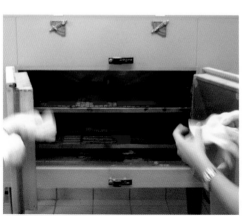

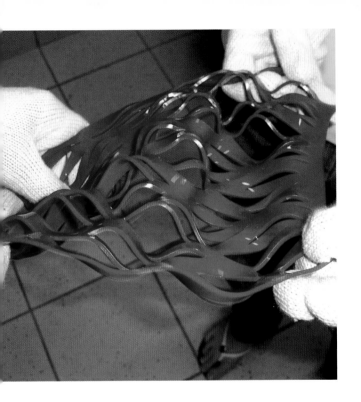

The ambition behind the design was to enhance an ordinary visit to the hairdressers with an illusionary feeling of glamour, inviting individual vanity and encouraging socializing. Within the space of the hair salon, theatricality was a means to transform the quotidian into the spectacular. The owner's demand for visual control as well as the necessity for clientele privacy instigated the idea of optical filtering devices suspended within a fluid space. Experimenting with the [cut-stretch] algorithm in paper and acrylic, I observed that sequences of slots in alternating rows resulted in an elastic condition of the surface that allowed three-dimensional curvature. I decided to develop this prototype into a series of porous screens responding to the problem of optical filtering in the hair salon. Linear incisions transformed into curvilinear openings affected by the weight of the surface itself when hanging. The first samples were done in canvas and then synthetic leather, a material resilient to tearing as well as sprayed hair products. The client's appeal for retro glamour coupled with an ironic resemblance of synthetic leather samples to hair dyes, leading to a colour palette of gold, silver, bronze, pink, white, and black vinyl.

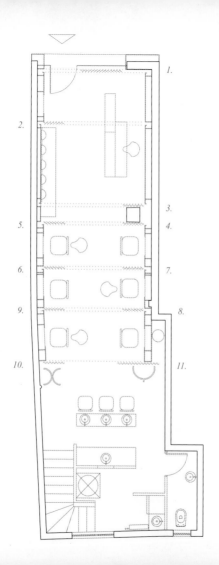

1.
2.
3.
4.
5.
6.
7.
8.
9.
10.
11.

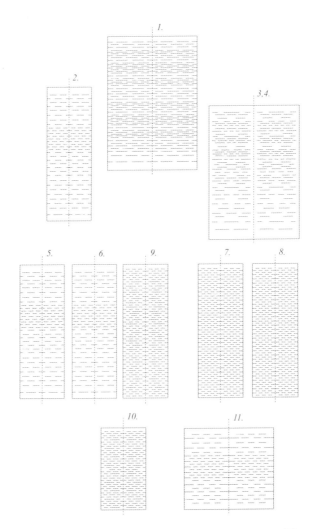

29

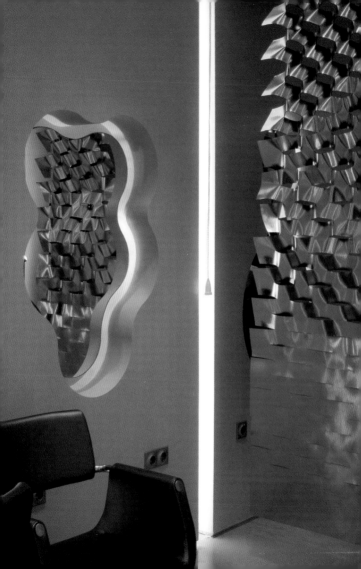

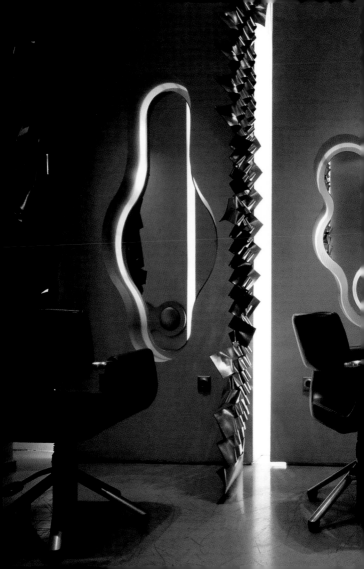

cut - enfold

The object explores form-generation opportunities in the minimum. Surface transformation occurs by folding the edges of a strip through an internal slot. Initial experiments were conducted in sheets of polyethylene Fibran. The prototype tested at the day nursery was a two-meter by one-meter flexible mat comprised of four layers of polyethylene and a core of plastic mesh. Children were excited and incorporated surface transformations in group play improvisations. They were stimulated by the capacity of the mat to enclose a small group, collapse, and recompose. Child play activities generated a variety of enfoldings; those noted include wear, cross, lie on, jump, bite, and toddle.

A regular pattern of parallel strips acquires formal complexity through a generative series of actions disciplined in time: cut, split, pleat, and fold. Pleated along the series of cuts, the object is folded twice. Expanding, the fold is distributed to each individual strip. The elementary component – made of opaline paper – is reproduced and assembled into a screen, functioning as an interior shading system. Variation is achieved through folding gestures upon each pleated component. Porosity occurs between adjacent strips. Velcro is used to adjust proximity between components and regulate larger openings.

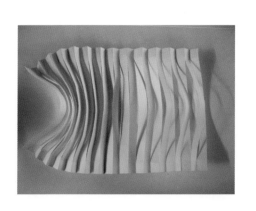

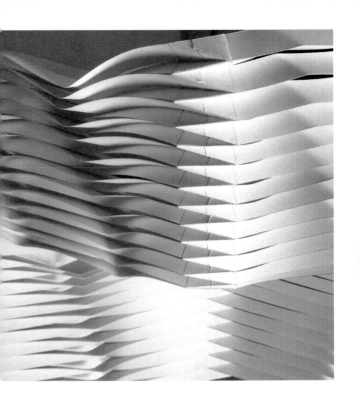

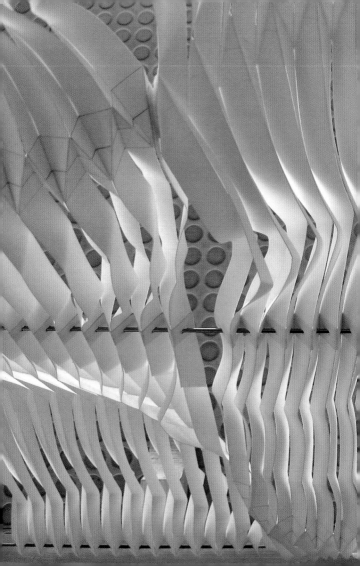

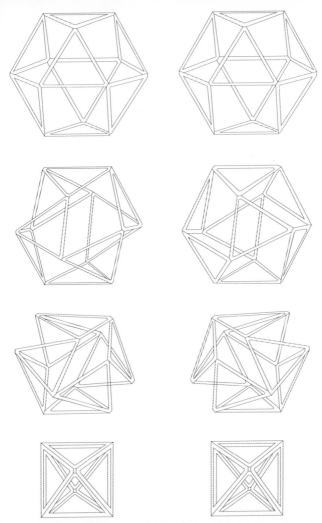

Olga Touloumi

Articulating Collapsible Universes

What is it that attracts us to shell structures and deployables? Geodesic domes, trusses, inflatables, foldables, pneumatics, and the like have been holding captive the imagination of thousands of aspiring architects around the world. Recent years have found deployables of all sizes, colors, and shapes popping up through the pages of architectural journals. We have seen screens folding and unfolding in space; patterns articulating themselves to infrastructural infinities; domes collapsing to unperceivable nothingnesses; and shells subsuming their orderly bodies to the entropic function of an all-devouring nature, or even emerging as the structured order to survive environmental noise. It seems as if the call for more sustainable and environmentally-friendly design in architects' minds directly translates to systemic architectures. But, what does it mean for architects to turn to deployables and shell structures amid growing anxieties over the future of the environment? What kind of economy do these engineered gimmicks suggest for architecture?

To begin with, the environment that these structures evoke starts with a team of industrialists, scientists, and bureaucrats invested in future studies, who met in the Accademia dei Lincei in Italy in 1968 to share their concern over the future of humanity and to decide upon their further actions. *(i)* After a two-week conference at MIT where Jay Forrester presented his System Dynamics method of analyzing and predicting the function of systems and their interlocking, the group that came to be known as the "Club of Rome" commissioned the group at the MIT Sloan School of Management to research growth and the factors that determine it. *(ii)* The problem proved to be a tough one. Since natural resources were finite and data showed growth to be exponential, the system was doomed to collapse unless the behavior of the components that partake in it and the ways in which they relate to one another changed. Hence, according to the Club of Rome humanity not only had to look into the environment and nature in terms of systems that interlock, but also to redesign their articulation for two entities working against each other: humans and nature.

Scientists were not the only ones to pose the problem of articulation in the engineering of systems. Buckminster Fuller was one of the first to investigate the topic in design. In 1970 Doxiadis invited him to a letter exchange that would eventually lead to the consolidation of the two megatheories of ekistics and synergetics. In the first sixteen unpublished pages of the sixty-nine page "Letter to Doxiadis," Fuller employed the example of a wasp that gets trapped inside a house with a half-opened window in order to discuss the predicament of two contiguous systems without a designed articulation. In his story, the entrapped wasp was doomed to death unless by pure chance it found the way out during one of its numerous flights towards the light that the invisible barrier of the window stopped violently. Of course, the anecdote was not to advocate for a "wasp-friendly" design, but rather to raise in what Bucky named "design science" the question of articulation between two "organisms" of different teleologies – that is, a house with windows to let in the light but not the cold, and a wasp that moves towards the light but cannot perceive the barrier of the window. *(iii)* In Bucky's synergetic universe where the behavior of the whole could not be predicted by the behavior of any of the parts separately, the success or the failure of the system depended on the workings of its articulations.

The problem of articulation troubled Fuller not only on the theoretical level, but also on the very level of architectural practice. The first two projects to launch him as an entrepreneur and designer, that is the 4D Tower *(iv)* and the 4D House, *(v)* opposed their prefabricated bodies to past construction methods and proposed an architecture that articulates itself ad hoc from nothingness to full existence. With the geodesic domes, he turned the issue of articulation from a structural problem to a geometric one. The final form of each of his domes depended equally on the pattern introduced by the geometry of the units and on the ways in which they articulate with one another. But for the most part, the American inventor found the design of joints to be integral to his research on collapsible structures. Already from his Dymaxion Map, *(vi)* Fuller imagined a universe that folds and unfolds at will, while with his Jitterbug *(vii)* that continuously transforms from an icosahedron to a octahedron to a tetrahedron, Bucky demonstrated in a very physical way his conviction that everything in his synergetic universe actually boils down to a simple tetrahedron. *(viii)* In short, Fuller persistently considered the condition of architecture within the context of dynamic articulations, the deployment of which would eventually take over the world, pretty much as his Dymaxion Deployment Unit delivered par avion in the Persian Gulf did. *(ix)* To be more precise, for him the question of articulation lay at the heart of the problem of architecture, while aesthetic sensibilities only came second to tectonics and structural solutions, if the former did not resulted from the latter. After all, Fuller derived his synergetics from geometry and believed design to be more of a science and less of an art.

Regardless of how blind or attentive to the discourse that has informed their engineered bodies and their history, deployables and shell structures emphatically present to architecture the same questions their ancestors posed to the field. They still derive their formalistic kicks from structural innovation; look to geometry for the methodology to inform their design research; and take pride in their ability to transform, adjust, and even collapse at times. The opportunity, however, that shells and deployables brought to architecture lies not in their adjustability and collapsibility, but rather in their capacity to articulate parts to wholes, systems to other systems. Maybe designers can finally now shake the inert body of architecture, as Bucky shook his Jitterbug, and allow for an economy of articulations to emerge. To focus on systems alone does not suffice, as it neglects the primary condition that allows a system to emerge: its articulations. After all, even architecture as a field takes place not in isolation, but in its articulation with other disciplines.

References:

(i)   Donella H. Meadows, Club of Rome., and Potomac Associates., *The Limits to Growth : A Report for the Club of Rome's Project on the Predicament of Mankind, 2d ed. (New York: Universe Books, 1974), ix.*
(ii)   *Ibid., xi.*

(iii)　　　Fuller, Buckminster, "Letter to Doxiadis, June 14, 1966," General Scientific Matters: Bucky Fuller (Correspondence and Working File) Folder II (Letter Substitution), Constantinos A. Doxiadis Archives.

(iv)　　　R. Buckminster Fuller, The Artifacts of R. Buckminster Fuller: A Comprehensive Collection of His Designs and Drawings vol. 1 (New York: Garland, 1985), R. Buckminster Fuller and James Ward, The Artifacts of R. Buckminster Fuller : A Comprehensive Collection of His Designs and Drawings (New York: Garland, 1985), 22.

(v)　　　Ibid., 58-59.

(vi)　　　R. Buckminster Fuller, "How to Assemble the Globe," Life, March 1943.

(vii)　　　R. Buckminster Fuller, The Artifacts of R. Buckminster Fuller: A Comprehensive Collection of His Designs and Drawings vol. 4 (New York: Garland, 1985) Fuller and Ward, The Artifacts of R. Buckminster Fuller : A Comprehensive Collection of His Designs and Drawings, 372-73.

(viii)　　　Buckminster Fuller designed the Jitterbug based on the vector equilibrium principle. This is one of the definitions he gave to the term: "Jitterbug: "Now I can't have six equilateral triangles around each corner because it would add up to 360o and the system would not come back on itself. So I have limitations. I can't have any less than three trianles to get this inside and outside. There are only three possible structural systems in the Universe: tetrahedron, octahedron, and icosahedron. As I pumped this closest-packed set of 12-around-one, it went down like that – it went down through the icosahedron phase – that's exactly what happened when you took one ball out – it goes through that, and then it becomes the octahedron. So this vector equilibrium pumps between the three possible cases of all structural systems. So you begin to see how it is the framework of how things happen in nature." See: Edgar Jarratt Applewhite, A Synergetics Dictionary: The Mind of Buckminster Fuller vol. 2 (New York: Garland Publications, 1986), 443.

(ix)　　　Fuller and Ward, The Artifacts of R. Buckminster Fuller : A Comprehensive Collection of His Designs and Drawings, 55.

Illustrations:

p 46　　　Jitterbug after Buckminster Fuller, drawing by Valentina Karga
p 49-50　　　Buckminster Fuller during the proceedings of the Delos Symposium Networks and the Human Settlements, Delos, 1970 Photograph © Constantinos and Emma Doxiadis Foundation.

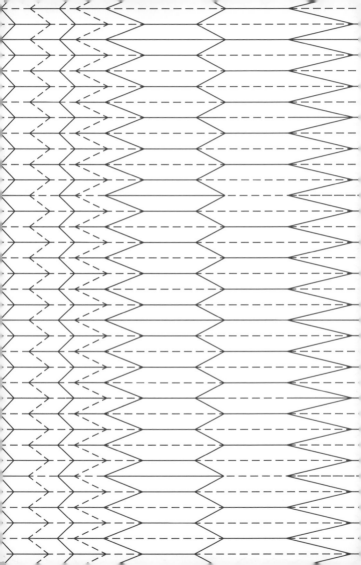

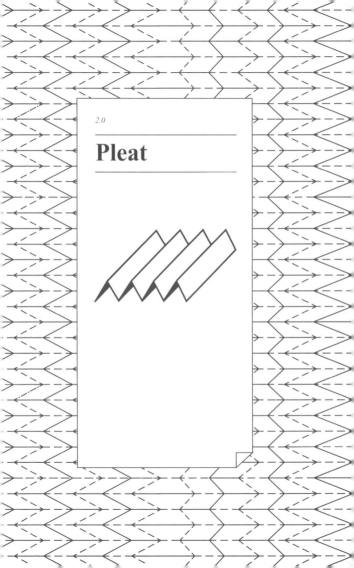

2.0

Pleat

 *fishbones*

The project explores variations of origami archetype miura-ori. Departing from the elementary pattern generator – a rectangle divided by one diagonal – arrays of oblique rectangles and rhomboids are produced. The potential of the pleated surface to enfold, producing concave and convex curvilinear spaces, is explored in ivory carton. A prototype is further produced as a deployable pleated shell using translucent nylon, plastic tape, and balsa wood rods. The collapsible frame is unresolved at the nodes, allowing a loose fit between edges and enabling a set of three postures: a pleated vault, a cocoon and a flat pack.

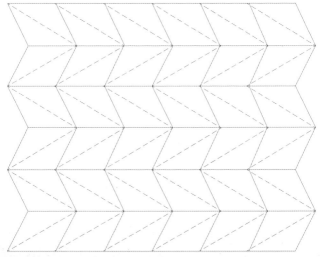

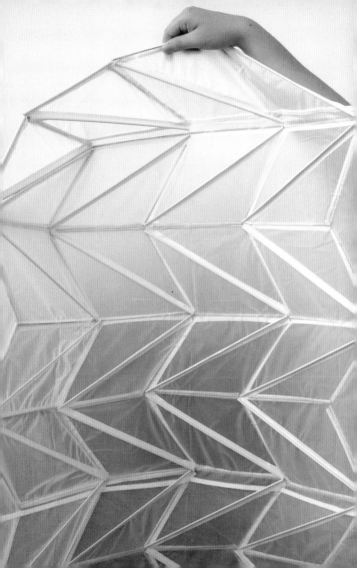

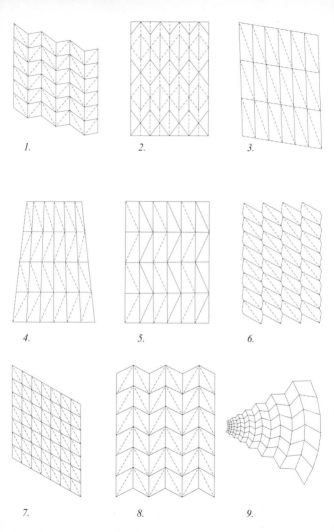

1. *2.* *3.*

4. *5.* *6.*

7. *8.* *9.*

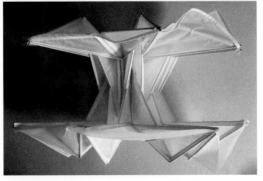

The project aims at the production of an emergency park strategically designed with the potential to transform within a few days into a settlement to shelter people affected by natural disasters. The proposed shelter unit is energy-efficient, recyclable, polymorphic and extendable, easy to transfer and install and engaging the dwellers in its construction process. It provides safety and the highest quality of living possible under the circumstances. Thermal comfort and individual floor area within the dwelling are considered as a set of minimum necessary conditions. The dwelling core is a self-supporting pleated tube to which deployable components – sleeping areas, veranda and bathroom – adhere. Dwelling parts are transported to the location by truck in flat packages and erected in situ. The pleated surface is multi-layered, including structural strata (honeycomb cardboard, Tectan board) and insulation strata (Actis, Gore-Tex). On its south-facing side, the hot air accumulated between the pleats can be released into the interior. Side and top facets can rotate into openings.

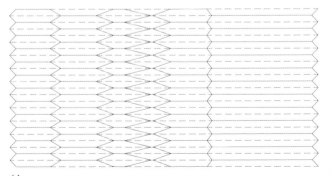

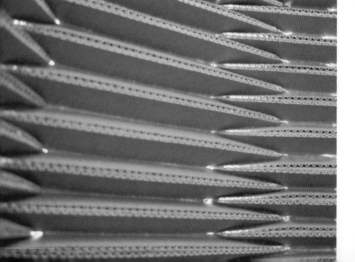

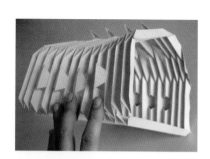

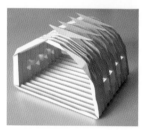

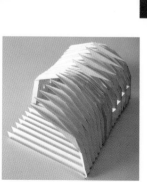

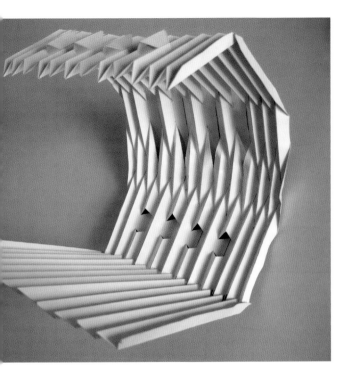

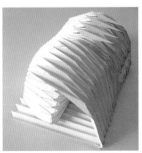

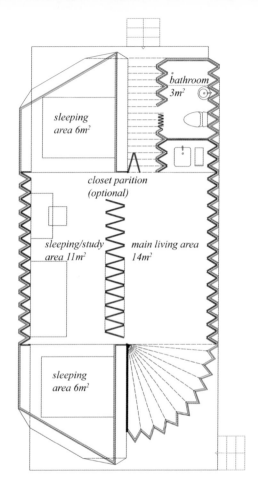

bathroom
3m²

sleeping
area 6m²

closet parition
(optional)

sleeping/study
area 11m²

main living area
14m²

sleeping
area 6m²

plan
expanded components

72

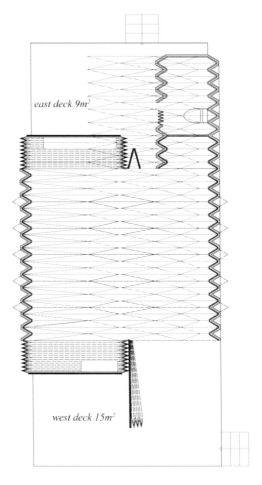

east deck 9m²

west deck 15m²

plan
packed components

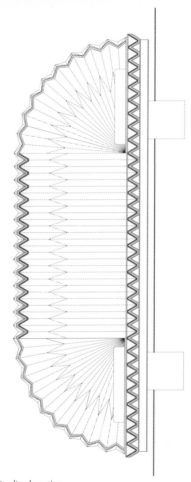

longitudinal section

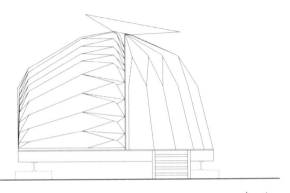

east elevation

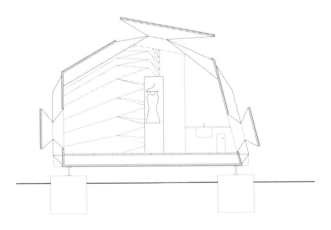

cross section

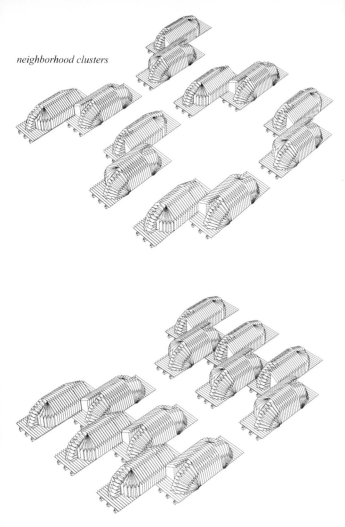

neighborhood clusters

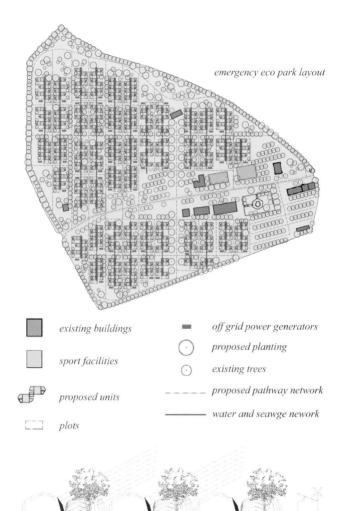

emergency eco park layout

existing buildings		off grid power generators	
sport facilities		proposed planting	
proposed units		existing trees	
plots		proposed pathway network	
		water and seawge nework	

The installation explores the potential of a pleated shell to become kinetic, achieving variable envelope configurations. The prototype is fabricated in corrugated cardboard and duct tape. Based on a symmetric fishbone pattern, the shell is cohesive and self-supporting. Form-finding is introduced as collective play within a small group. There are two noteworthy limits in this indeterminate series of transformations: flat packaging that allows transportation to location and enfolding that produces a minimum inhabitable capsule. In between, play constantly affects the animated envelope, informing and deforming it.

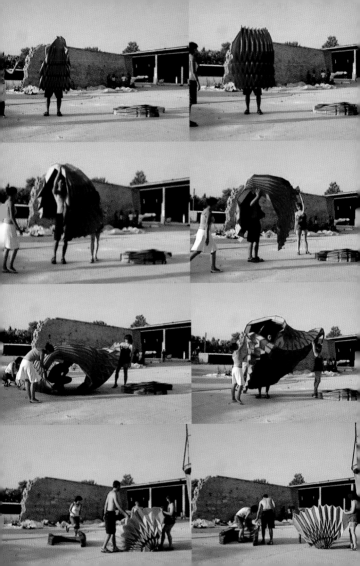

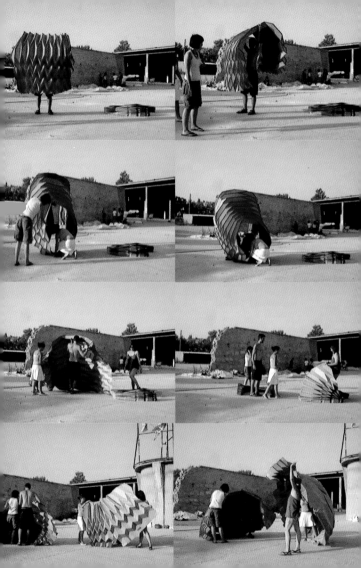

The elemental pleat is composed of four adjoining edges, three mountain folds and one valley. Its serial array produces one pleated strip. Rotating, its beginning meets its end, forming an annulus – a pleated hollow cylinder. This further revolves around its vertical axis, retrieving two static postures: a convex one forming a dome and a concave one forming a semi-torus. The first kinetic prototype is fabricated in corrugated cardboard and incorporated as a prop in a theatrical improvisation. A more complex pattern is later developed into a collapsible backpack. The pattern is divided into cardboard facets held together with cotton elastane.

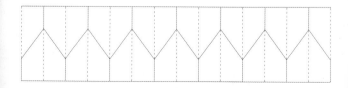

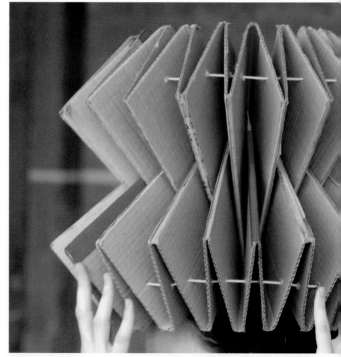

 *pleat - tile*

Once the diagonals of a square become mountain folds, a pyramid is generated. Folding the altitudes of its triangular faces into valleys, the pyramid is pleated. Orthogonal array of the pleated pyramid in alternating rows generates an articulated assembly that can perform as one surface. The prototype is fabricated in grey 2mm cardboard. This kinetic and polymorphic surface can contract and expand, acquire multiple curvatures, become a dome or a vault, and fold back into a flat pack.

ΚΑΤΑΣΚΕΥΗ ΜΑΚΕΤΑΣ

ΜΟΝΑΔΑ   ΠΑΤΡΟΝ

ΚΟΡΥΦΗ

ΚΟΙΛΑΔΑ

Πολλαπλασιασμός μονάδας και εφαρμογή υλικού

Igor P. Siddiqui

Surface Fatigue

In materials science, fatigue is a type of failure mode that occurs when particular external forces are repeatedly exerted over a surface, resulting in material degradation. Over time, a smooth surface is progressively transformed and weakened by the accumulation of localized microscopic cracks, until a particular crack reaches a critical size and causes structural failure. *(i)* The material surface, in other words, grows tired as it is exposed to repeated external demands, its area subdivided by striations and reorganized into a tessellating micro-pattern. In contemporary architecture, surface has enjoyed a privileged status as a popular subject of morphogenetic research as well as a generator of spatial organization and affect. Digital design technologies, in particular surface-based modeling software, have over the past two decades unleashed the plastic capacity of architectural surfaces to nimbly respond to external factors, while facilitating a range of potent techniques for constructing connectivity and continuity within and across spatial, material and informational differences. Generated digitally, the contemporary surface is ubiquitous and seemingly omnifunctional, with a performance repertoire that demands extensive multitasking: skin, structure, aperture, interior atmosphere, furnishings, fenestration, landscape. Reflecting the evolving integration of digital tools in the architectural design process, from scripting to fabrication, as well as in response to issues of scale, constructability and material, the surface that may have once been continuous, monolithic, and smooth, has progressively become patterned, component-based, and striated. *(ii)*

Scanning the broad range of digitally generated projects of the past decade, from gallery installations to sports stadiums, it appears that the contemporary surface gains vitality through panelization, tessellating, and subdivision. These patterns, frequently ornamental in appearance, provide the means and methods for the architectural manifestation of the surface at full-scale, including geometric rationalization, part-to-whole organization, and material distribution. By freely associating the surface patterns that emerge through material behavior with those that are generated digitally at the scale of architectural components, one arrives to an evolving body of work by contemporary designers whose inquiries target the intersection between material self-organization and digital automation. Varied in motivation – from emulating dynamic material conduct at the micro-scale as a means of diagrammatically scripting architectural formation over time to engaging with particular material properties for their form-finding potential – such work expands the agency that materials have in the design process, accepting them neither as passive receivers of preconceived form nor as static entities with fixed behavior. While the digital surface in contemporary architecture has been showing signs of fatigue for quite some time now – overexposed, overworked, spread too thin, and allover exhausted – a recent crop of digitally-minded designers and design educators, Sophia Vyzoviti among them, have been reinvigorating the tired surface by embracing its expanded repertoire of material performance. Vyzoviti's porous and deployable architectural screens, much like the work of her contemporaries that include Atelier Manferdini, Matsys, Hirsuta, and ISSSStudio, exploit materials' response to and interaction with factors such as gravity, time, and human participation, and consider materiality as a dynamic condition made static only through temporal framing. The resulting surfaces are organized by various patterns of aggregation and their three-dimensional manifestation, contingent upon deployment at full-scale, resists a priori representation. By inextricably linking rule-based pattern geometries, material behaviors as well as human and environmental prompts to one another, the projects effectively compress the conventional distance between studio-based design processes and their site-deployed outcomes.

In his essay "Material Complexity", *(iii)* Manuel DeLanda argued that materials' morphogenetic potential is best expressed by their complex and variable behavior. In defining the aspirations relative to the relationship between form and material, DeLanda's following statement captures the kinds of ambitions that resonate throughout much of the work under consideration:

We may now be in a position to think about the origin of form and structure, not as something imposed from the outside on an inert matter, not as a hierarchical command from above as in an assembly line, but as something that may come from within the materials, a form that we tease out of those materials as we allow them to have their say in the structures we create. *(iv)*

Such a position, in the context of digital design, suggests a reciprocal power dynamic between computational and material means, resisting in this way the technocratic top-down approach to form-making. Rather than resorting to relentless patterning as a digital method of disciplining materiality, projects such as Matsys' P_ Wall (2009) *(vi)* recognize materials' active agency in the plastic formation of the architectural surface. The project, a room-sized wall-mounted museum installation, consists of a series of tessellated hexagonal pan-

Matsys, P_Wall

els whose geometries are informed by the interaction of the liquid plaster from which they were cast with the formwork used for the casting. The overall surface is organized by two overlaid digitally generated patterns: the rhythmically differentiated hexagonal field and a point-field. Together, the two provide the geometries that define the formwork for casting, which in turn determines the constraints within and against which the plaster behaves. When cured, the hardened panels capture the dynamic behavior of the liquid material as it encounters the digitally calibrated geometries, the materiality of the formwork and the influences of gravity and time. The temporal aspect of material performance is further amplified in Hirsuta's Raspberry Fields (2008–present), *(vii)* a house renovation that includes new exterior cladding designed to progressively reflect the environmental forces exerted onto its surface. The house is clad in wood, and each wood tile – shingle – is designed contrary to the convention whereby the wood grain is parallel to the long side of each tile in order to minimize material deformation. Instead, the grain is oriented to maximize, rather than suppress, the geometric transfor-

Hirsuta, Raspberry Fields

Atelier Manferdini, West Coast Pavilion

mation of the flat material as an effect of weathering. With the passage of time, the shingles are expected to progressively curl, twist and tangle, more or less depending on their position in relation to the prevailing wind and storm direction. The evolving form of the building envelope - thickened, furry, and geometrically relaxed - is a result of the material's range of responses to localized external forces within the constraints of the tiling pattern. The surface also gets relaxed and as such performs more effectively in Atelier Manferdini's West Coast Pavilion (2006). *(v)* The temporary structure's envelope, organized by a matrix of nesting polygons, is digitally cut from sheet metal and consists of a series of interlaced components, part taut part draped. The draping is a result of the subtractive process that produces apertures across the flat surface as the material that would ordinarily be removed is allowed to cling on and is reattached to the structure in order to further articulate the envelope through texture, detail and modulation of light. Calystegia (2010) by ISSSStudio, a wall/curtain hybrid, exploits the draping of wool felt as a method of calibrating surface aperture. Based on a parametric array of components, the behavior of soft felt transforms the form of 'hard' digital geometry, introducing to the computationally based gradient of openings an overlay

ISSSStudio, Calystegia

of apertures that are an outcome of the system's interaction with gravity. What is perceived in the digital model as a single closed seam between adjacent components in fact splits open once the prototype is physically installed perpendicularly to the ground plane. The resulting openings are inversely proportional to those with the adjacent components – the smaller the opening within, the larger the split in-between. Digital computation and material calibration produce a range of mutually dependent surface conditions that modulate view, filter light and intensify the textural quality of the double-sided interior screen.

Within this context, Sophia Vyzoviti's collaborative work with students further articulates the design-research trajectories pursued by her international peers as it engages with the complex relationships between design techniques, forms and materials. To a degree that is greater than her colleagues, however, Vyzoviti explicitly reintroduces the body as central to the process. Surveying the extensive documentation of her most recent series of investigations – the porous and deployable screens – one encounters architectural form contingent upon the active presence of fingers, hands, arms, torsos, full figures, even multiple bodies. In a self-described low-tech/high-concept manner, *(viii)* the collaborative bodies enable the emergence of adaptable soft shells by providing the interface between rule-based geometric patterns and flexible material properties. In this way, the bodies act as agents of systematic design techniques, and are also frequently used as the projects' site and program. The documentation of the work, as framed by the book, is organized in four sections: cut, pleat, tile, and weave. The title of each section is both a noun and a verb, referring to the repeated pattern unit that is embedded within each porous screen on the one hand, but also the action through which each flat material surface is transformed into a thickened architectural condition on the other. Each cutting, pleating, tiling and weaving pattern is spatialized and three-dimensionalized by iterative handwork, with the bodies at once reaffirming and dismantling the rigid repetition of the pattern geometries. Not unlike the rock band described in Dave Hickey's essay "The Delicacy of Rock-and-Roll", the collective bodies produce, despite their focused precision, a "a hurricane of noise, this infinitely complicated, fractal filigree of delicate distinction." *(ix)* What is revealed in the surface noise of apertures, folds, and ribbons is a range within which surface components – both in relation to their individual geometries as well as relative to their position within the overall system – can produce variation. The pattern is both a set of repeated geometries and a series of actions and the body mediates between predetermined form and material behavior.

Frequently supplementing these primary patterns/actions are secondary instructions (e.g. cut-stretch, cut-fold), which invite the participants to intervene within the emergent geometries through pure action – no preconceived pattern. By stretching, twisting and revolving the perforated, folded and woven material, the bodies act as forces of tension and compression and, by providing the variables of space and time to each construction, effectively serve as the projects' sites. While the body-as-site intent is explicit given several of the wearable constructions in the collection, it is the participants' exertion of force over the materials in order to observe and record their formal behavior that particularly blurs the clear distinction between the space of the designer and the site of deployment, and thus between the design process and its outcome. In installations like Meanderplex the scaling up of model-making materials such as paper to the architectural full-scale too blurs the distinction between process and product. Along with the rational rules of engagement and the negotiation of the group dynamic, the paper's incremental movement, sagging, and warping – the material's demonstration of fatigue as a result of overworking – reveals an expanded range of the system's morphogenetic potential. The constructed paper screen, an aggregation of multiple components by multiple bodies installed as an interior gallery facade, is both a form-finding instrument and an architectural product that is responsive to its spatial program.

Vyzoviti's practice –indeed the experimental, iterative and improvisational quality of the work delightfully reminds one more of band or dance practice than of conventional architectural labor – while thoroughly informed by the theoretical and technological content of digital practice, eschews the architectural limits of computation by investing in and constantly renewing the relationships between human participation and material agency. At a moment when various computational platforms are promising thorough informational integration from design to construction, material behavior is reduced to digital scripts, and architects are (for good reason) increasingly invested in code-writing, her extensive body of work is a reminder of the generative potential of design processes that occur in the spaces that are interstitial, tangential, marginal, but nevertheless deeply related to digital practice. By pairing the performative repertoire of participating designers with the range of behaviors of materials, Vyzoviti's differentiated surfaces reflect - not as a matter of value judgment, but rather as a source of expanded potential – a spectrum of "energy levels" from extreme fitness to slouchy fatigue. The practice as such focuses on the organization of labor in relation to material organization and, rather than repressing, amplifies as a matter of research and insight the expanded range of behaviors outside of static states of equilibrium. In Vyzoviti's work as well as in that of her like-minded contemporaries, the emphasis is not, to echo DeLanda again, "on the spontaneous generation of form" *(x)* nor is it a matter of maintaining a position outside of digital practice; instead, such experimental efforts seek to forge new affirmative relationships between computation, materiality and the designer and as such rescue the contemporary surface from cliché.

References:

(i) I am indebted to my colleague Damon Northrop for his feedback and insight during our productive exchanges about material behavior in relation to surface fatigue.

(ii) Branko Kolarevic and Kevin Klinger, "Manufacturing / Material / Effects," in Manufacturing Material Effects: Rethinking Design and Making in Architecture, ed. Branko Kolarevic et al. (New York: Routledge, 2008), 13.

(iii) Manuel DeLanda, "Material Complexity," in Digital Tectonics, ed. Neil Leach et al. (West Sussex: Wiley-Academy, 2004), 20.

(iv) Ibid, 21.

(v) "P_Wall (2009)," Matsys, accessed November 9, 2010, http://matsysdesign.com/category/projects/p_wall2009/.

(vi) "Raspberry Fields," Hirsuta, accessed November 9, 2010, http://www.hirsuta.com/RASP.html; also, "Raspberry Fields," SuckerPUNCH, posted on January 18, 2010, http://www.suckerpunchdaily.com/2010/01/18/raspberry-fields/.

(vii) Lisa Iwamoto, Digital Fabrications: Architectural and Material Techniques (New York: Princeton Architectural Press, 2009), 42-46. Additional project information is available on the designer's website http://ateliermanferdini.com.

(viii) Sophia Vyzoviti, "From paperfolds to object-space prototypes," in Supersurfaces: Folding as a method of generating forms for architecture, products and fashion (Amsterdam: BIS Publishers, 2006), 10.

(ix) Dave Hickey, "The Delicacy of Rock-and-Roll," in Air Guitar: Essays on Art & Democracy (Los Angeles: Art issues. Press, 1997), 101.

(x) DeLanda,19.

3.0

Tile

folded brickwork

This architectural detail was developed as a strategy for formal assimilation in the development of a new housing and shopping complex in the KM area of downtown Athens. The prototype presented here in Canson paper was intended to be made of terracotta. Assembled into a large porous façade, the ceramic pixel aimed at establishing formal and material continuity with its urban context, abounding in characteristics typical of vernacular neoclassic buildings in Athens' historic centre, while at the same time creating a novel identity for the urban block. The formal vocabulary involved in the creation of the folded component drew from Hellenic ceramics as well as local façade decoration. The ceramic screen encloses the urban block's semi-public spaces – the circulation system and collective sports facilities. Its porous constitution tempers sunlight, operating as a bioclimatic device, orientation signage, and environmental ornament.

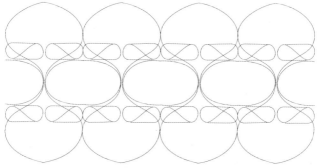

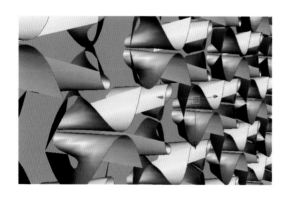

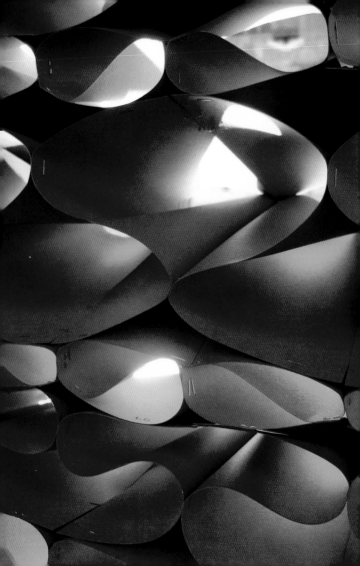

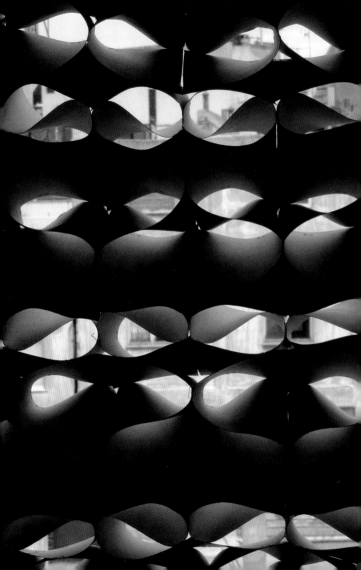

Topological archetype and favourite architectural metaphor, the Mobius strip, is treated here as a component of a supersurface. Strips of varying width are paired in triangles and tiled into rhomboids. The prototype is fabricated in 250 g/m2 opaline paper. This porous screen was temporarily installed in an abandoned factory. Filtering daylight and casting nocturnal shadows, it offered environmental ornament, emulating a foliage effect in contrast with its industrial setting.

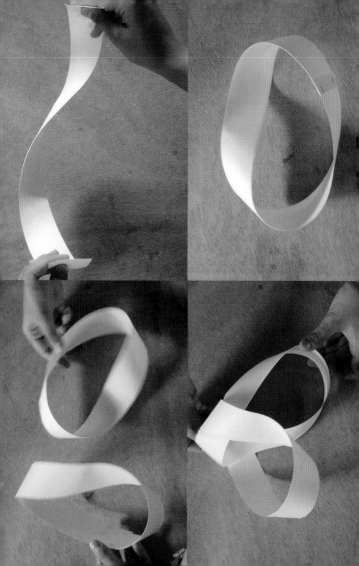

An array of four squares pleated along their diagonals forms the elementary component of this surface – a pleated strip. Each strip is closed, producing a collapsible polygon of eight faces. Assembly of components is established by flexible joints – squares pleated along one diagonal. Prototypes were fabricated in Shoeller paper, PVC and polypropylene. The screen is kinetic: its porosity is adjusted as components contract and expand. It can be used as interior partitioning or shading system. Velcro is used for fixtures.

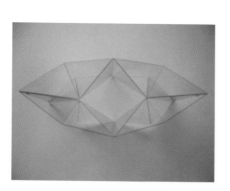

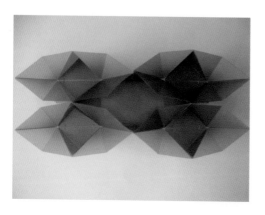

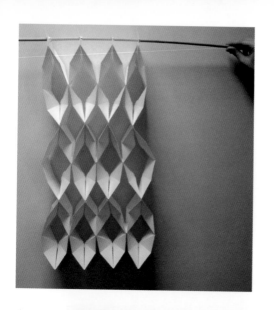

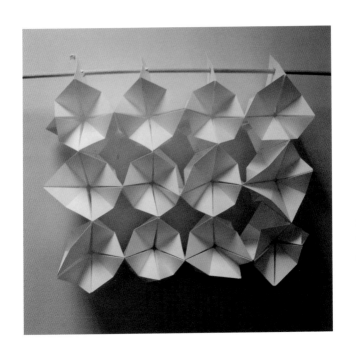

137

rhomboids

The elementary component generating the three-dimensional pattern is a pleated rhomboid split in half. Arrays in alternating rows produce tiles which can be repeated ad infinitum. The rhomboids screen was commissioned by a major publishing house in Athens to refurbish their headquarters. The aim behind the design was to demonstrate sculptural qualities of paper, at the same time providing sustainable corporate décor. This lightweight screen was handcrafted in sheets of 220g/m2 opaline paper and magnetically affixed to the existing cubicle partitioning system. It enclothed the meeting room and part of the reception area, establishing visual continuity between the two.

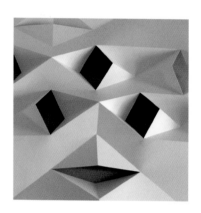

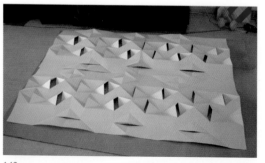

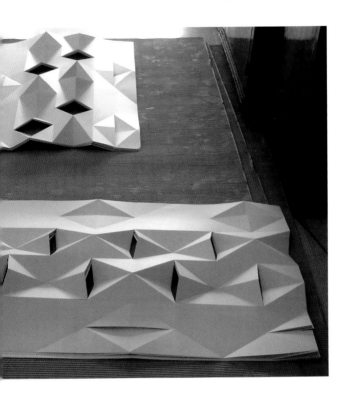

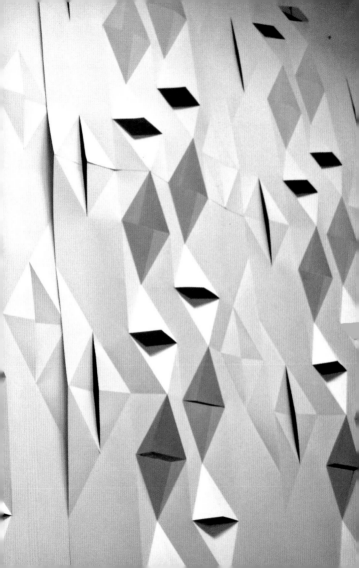

The elementary component of this screen is generated through consecutive enfoldings of a surface striated by an orthogonal grid. Components are regularly tiled and held together by an invisible grid framed to fit. Initial experiments involved consecutive enfoldings of paper and aluminium sheets. The prototype was designed as an interior partition and fabricated in150g/m2 opaline paper immersed in paraffin.

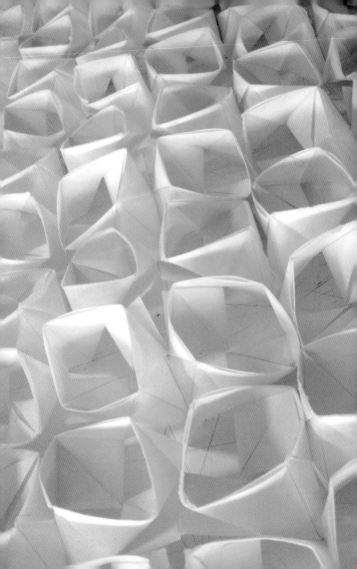

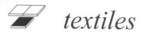 *textiles*

The geometry of the surfaces relies on regular tiling of self-intersecting strips, each one affixed to its immediate neighbours. Individual units are porous and deployable, granting flexibility and permeability to surface as whole. Prototypes were fabricated from foam rubber and carpet fabric. The ones presented share the capacity to wrap and enclothe. Material softness renders them suitable for close contact with the body, to be used as garments.

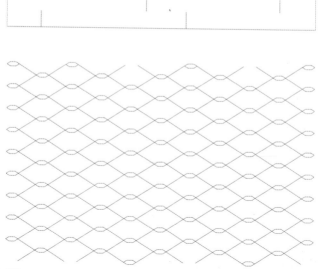

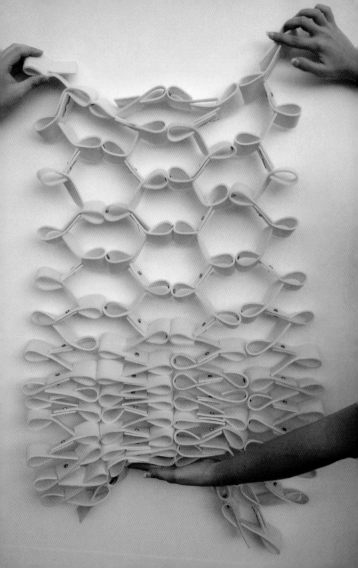

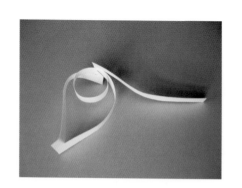

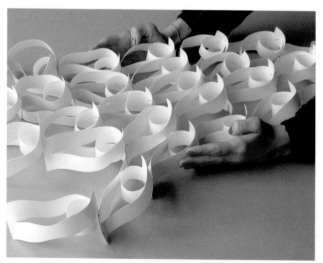

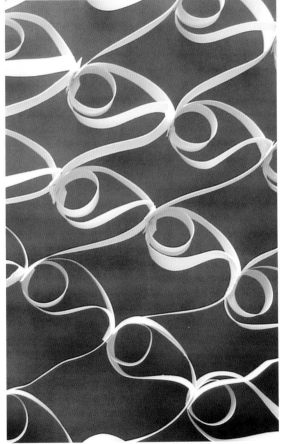

Sophia Vyzoviti

Participatory Form-finding

Some years ago in Singapore, I was excited to observe group paper-folding sessions taking place in the park of the condominium where I was staying. Under a large tent sheltering a paper altar, grown-ups and children gathered around tables, prolifically folding through stacks of decorated paper. Coloured orange and yellow, clad in gold, or inscribed in red, what turned out to be Chinese ceremonial funeral paper was folded into hollow cylinders and pyramids representing bars of gold or ancient coins. The event was in fact part of a Chinese wake, where friends and family accumulate ritualistic paper folds to be burnt in the funeral pyre in honour of the deceased, symbolically providing them with spending money for their journey in the underworld. This ritualistic paper craft, exotic to European eyes, I perceived as an allegory of a temporary creative community. Of course process and product in this case acquire meaning within a burial ritual; paper is used symbolically here, as it is associated with the sacred in East Asian culture. *(i)* Nevertheless, I observed that elementary form generation knowledge was exchanged within the group in terms of hands-on, practical geometric generation. Employing these simple rules, the group produced a large amount of artefacts that shared formal characteristics. The dynamics of this event, the collective production of ceremonial paper folds, culminating in their spectacular consumption in the funeral pyre, evoked a potential soft architectural project, a transient installation that would engage hand craft and collective form generation.

Morphogenetic research presented in 'Soft Shells: Porous and Deployable Architectural Screens' focuses on physical modelling of single-surface transformations, and particularly on their capacity to produce certain topological and morphological automata. A state-of-the-art definition of the research agenda conforms to Patrick Schumacher's notion of 'material computing'. Schumacher defines this as "analogue form-finding processes that can complement the new digital design tools and that might in fact be described as quasi-physical form-finding processes". *(ii)*

In my opinion, material form-finding devices – such as surface transformations through folding – retain their autonomy. Not only do they complement digital form-finding, but they also generate challenges: unprecedented and complex forms of material substance that yet remain to be modelled in silico. Their production relies on hand-mind coordination, where the intelligence of the hand mediates between topology and material. Their morphogenetic algorithms can be narrated. They can easily be conveyed as design knowledge, surface transformation instructions in sets of simple rules. Besides their design-generative capacity as material diagrams, paper folds could also be investigated as a shared formal vocabulary offering opportunities to scaffold collective creativity, as participatory form-finding devices.

Indeed, the field of architecture has a long history of participation. Alexander Tzonis demarcates the origins of collaboration between architects and the users of architecture in public debates concerning the Golden Age temples of the Athenian democracy. *(iii)* In the 20th century, participation was developed as a design strategy during the 1960s and 1970s and applied in practice by architects such as Chares Moore, Lucien Kroll, and Herman Hertzberger. Participation today is primarily employed in engaging local communities in the resolution of urban design problems.

The ideology of participation criticises the professional authority of the architect from the perspective of the inhabitant. Practical aspects of participatory design engage with the invention of design tools supporting communication between architects and users enabling the translation of negotiations in architectural terms. My concern lies in expanding participation within the architectural community, challenging the notion of authorship, and opening up architectural design process towards group dynamics. As my focus is on form-finding, I would like to explore the formation of a formal vocabulary which can be shared between creative individuals.

British sculptor Antony Gormley has been employing participatory form-finding since 1991 in his series of public art pieces Field. Working with communities around the globe, including Mexico, Brazil, China, and the UK, Gormley produces large-scale installations comprised of aggregates of elemental human figures made of clay. In the making of Asian Field – the largest installation in the series – he engaged the entire village of Xiangshan, a community of 350 people in the outskirts of Guangzhou in South China. Under his guidance, 190,000 little figures were made, consuming 25 tonnes of clay in the course of one week; the figures were baked in kilns at the local brick-making factory. (iv) The piece was initially exhibited occupying a space that was non-standard for art venues, the underground car park of a new residential development cluster in Guangzhou. The project has been discussed (v) as a totemic 'collective representation' and a place-making 'earthwork' evoking solidarity and collective identity. The making of Gormley's Field engages many areas of participation. What I find particularly interesting – discussing morphogenetic processes – is the systemisation of elementary design knowledge in a set of simple rules that can be appropriated by an entire community. The form-finding language of the elementary Asian Field component – the terracotta figurine – consisted of three basic rules:

a.   all figures had to be hand-sized and fit comfortably in one hand;

b.   all figures had to stand upright;

c.   all figures had to have two eyes gazing at a point above the horizon.

Generating a population of 190,000 elements by a set of three simple rules may operate as a provocative statement in the current architectural debate on parametricism: the systematic, adaptive variation of continuous differentiation and dynamic, parametric figuration. *(vi)*

'Meanderplex' *(vii)* is a recent project that I orchestrated in order to investigate participatory form-finding in the context of architectural education. The research question in this case can be formulated as follows: If form generation becomes an open and collective project, then can a shared repository of forms be established by systematic sets of simple rules? Based on a model of workshop teaching, 'meanderplex' developed around three cycles: individual form generation within a shared formal vocabulary, co-creation of a large-scale installation, and individual prototype development appropriating elements of the collective product.

[e1,s3]+
[e2,s2]-
[e2,s4]-

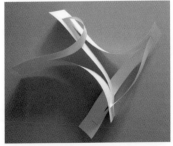

In the morphogenetic phase, a versatile prototype selected for its capacity to generate multiple variations was submitted to the group. The prototype illustrated the transformation of a meandering strip into a knot and was presented as an instructive plan and a generative sequence of intersections. In the second phase, each participant was provided opaline paper and asked to produce variations, noting for each one the generative sequence of intersections as directed pairs of slots and edges. Participants were introduced to the concept of variability within an object series, observing a population of objects deriving from one versatile paradigm. While this phase encompassed individual study, group cohesion was maintained by a shared formal vocabulary. In the third phase, participants created a collective archive of all variations produced, denoting the form-defining algorithm on an image of each component. Participants were asked to reproduce their most successful ones and contribute to the collective construct. Intuitive clusters were formed by interweaving individual components. A mega-cluster emerged additively, as the assembly proceeded in suspension. Interweaving was enabled by uniformity of joints between components. In the next phase, parallax object generation and assembly process were edited into a film distributed to all participants. *(viii)* Documentation of the event became the first product of this collective form-finding process.

The 'meanderplex' workshop was instigated by an invitation to exhibit the developments in my academic research in the context of 'The Archive_ Episodes'. *(ix)* In response, I designed 'meanderplex' as an installation that would demonstrate research processes as well as material outcomes responding to the particular spatial qualities of venue. 'Meanderplex' was represented as a collective form generation, as a commentary on analogue parametrics displaying an archive of serial variability, and as a product; a soft, porous paper screen suspended in the front window of 'The Archive'. Following the exhibition, 'meanderplex' returned to the academic studio as an open case for further development. Working alone or in pairs, students were able to select modules from the collective object log and construct a porous screen clustering multiple copies of one or two 'meanderplex' components. The new clusters were further treated as two-dimensional pattern generators and entered a new cycle of form-generation processes.

What constitutes the core of a creative community? Let's perform a paradigm shift and consider the community formed around the practice of skateboarding. According to Ian Borden, the nature of skateboarding as a practice is collective, not only because skaters enjoy skating together in 'sessions' – "a kind of informal competition among individuals that sometimes takes place under socially aggressive circumstances", *(x)* but also because individual skaters share a palette of achievable moves. Transcribing the constituents of this collective platform into the elemental task of architecture that is form-finding, we can derive two necessary conditions that may bind a group of architecture students into a creative community: working together in creative sessions towards a collective product and sharing a palette of achievable forms. 'Meanderplex' maintained equilibrium between heterogeneity and integrity. Surface variability was established through systematic articulation of sets of simple rules. As a participatory form-finding scaffold, it managed to sustain group cohesion between creative individuals. A collective reservoir of form generation narratives attracted depositing and loaning. The group's shared formal vocabulary has become public. Explicitly represented in terms of process, 'meanderplex' gained value through its capacity to narrate its origination and development. It formulated a case of an open process and an open product, a pending invitation to participate.

References:

(i)   On the oru-kami blog, for instance, we are informed that "paper has been associated with the sacred since papermaking was introduced to Japan from China via Korea in the fifth century. Cut paper was carried by travellers to ward off any evil spirits on their journeys. Cut paper forms with special writing were also carried to ward off evil spirits." Source http://en.oru-kami.net/blog/katashiro-when-paper-becomes-divine/ (accessed 9-3-2011)

(ii)   Patrik Schumacher, (2007) 'Engineering Elegance', in: Hanif Kara (editor), Design Engineering, London, AKT, http://www.patrikschumacher.com/Texts/Engineering%20Elegance.html (accessed 28-1-2011)

(iii)   Alexander Tzonis (2004) 'Participatory design: Needs, System, Paradox' in Hoang-Ell Jeng (editor), participation.tw, Taipei, Gardencity publishing

(iv)   http://www.antonygormley.com

(v)   WJT Mitchell, 'What Sculpture Wants: Placing Antony Gormley' in http://www.antonygormley.com (accessed 14-3-2011

(vi)   Patrik Schumacher (2008) 'Parametricism - A New Global Style for Architecture and Urban Design' in: AD Architectural Design - Digital Cities, Vol 79, No 4, July/August 2009, guest editor: Neil Leach, http://www.patrikschumacher.com/Texts/Parametricism%20as%20Style.htm (accessed 14-3-2011)

(vii)   w'Meanderplex' is included in the 'weave' chapter of 'Soft Shells'.

(vii)   Documentation is available online and can be accessed at www.supersurfaces-supersurfaces.blogspot.com

(ix)   The Archive Episodes is an event hosted by Carteco Design Center and curated by K&K architects. Information on the exhibition particulars can be accessed online at www.thearchive.gr.

(ix)   Individual developments are included in the 'weave' chapter of 'Soft Shells'.

(x)   Ian Borden (2003) Skateboarding, Space and the City- Architecture and the Body. Oxford-New York: Berg, pp.123.

Weave

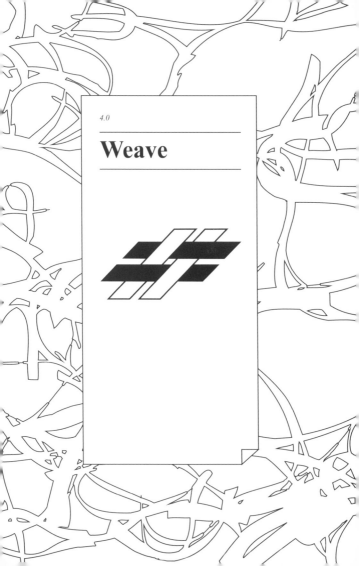

In current morphogenetic jargon, 'meanderplex' could be described as a parametric form study in analogue media. A population of parallax objects is derived from one meander strip employing simple rules of self-intersecting. For each one, form generation is formally described as hands-on knot theory, through directed pairs of edges and slots, perforations executed in disciplined sequences. Within each, curvilinearity is a physical automaton, a product of the ruse-based analogue machine. The overall form is a mega-cluster of interwoven components, a retro-futuristic weave. Component formation and assembly abide by the same rules of interweaving. Prototypes and installation cluster were fabricated in 220g/m2 opaline paper.

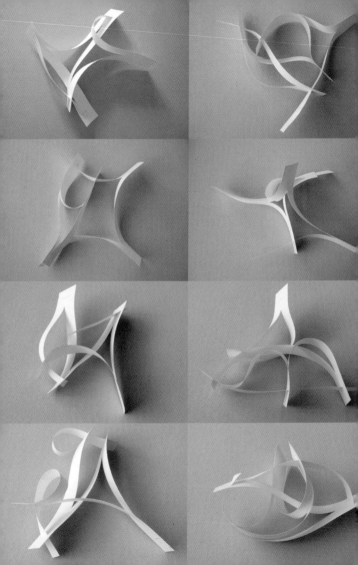

ween
ing a choice
not having one
use the first.

a novel way to approach architecture, design
studio like refuge, create, inspire, be inspired, present, exhibit,
simply esca... with clients

...thearchive.gr

ARCHIVE

 *pattern to relief*

Pattern generation initiates with a digital image fragment of a regular 'meanderplex' cluster. The fragment is subjected to the regular plane transformation of mirror symmetry. A vector drawing of the new pattern is then layered through offsets. Laser cutting and stacking introduces a recessed third dimension, raising the pattern to relief. The prototype is fabricated in grey cardboard.

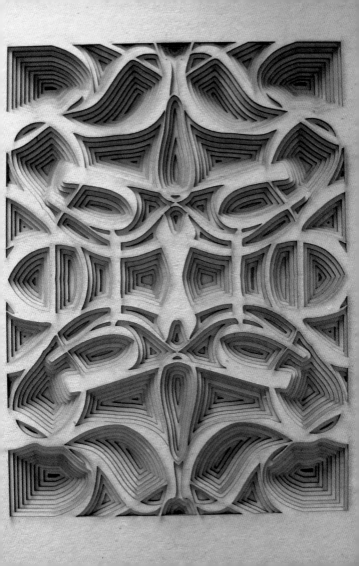

unit

↓

cluster

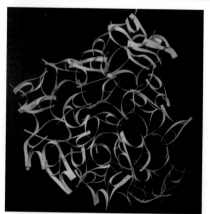

stack

↑

cut ◀

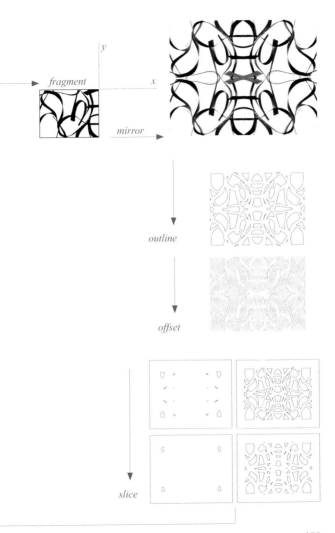

fragment

y

x

mirror

outline

offset

slice

189

Pattern generation initiates with a digital image fragment of a regular 'meanderplex' cluster. A bitmap of the fragment is replicated within an additive growth sequence. A vector drawing of the aggregate pattern is trimmed to a triangle which becomes an icosahedron's face. Truncated and unfolded, the icosahedron shrinks into a deployable pyramid. The prototype is fabricated through laser cutting in ivory carton.

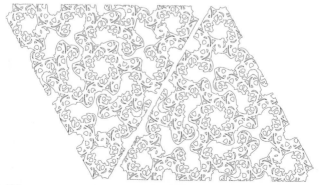

unit

↓

cluster

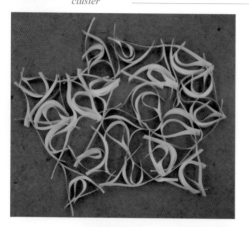

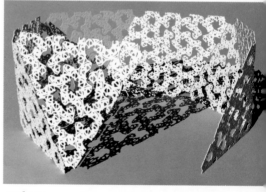

perforate   ◄

192

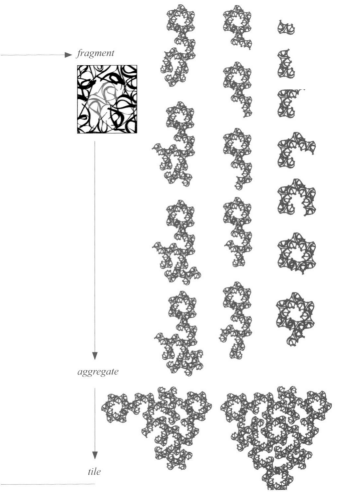

fragment

aggregate

tile

193

Multiple copies of two 'meanderplex' components are interwoven into a porous screen. Pattern generation initiates with a digital image of the cluster. A vector drawing of the cluster is further processed in Rhino. Its outline is lofted to a teardrop curve producing a rippling dome. The pattern extracted from the physical cluster flows along the rippling digital surface, reproducing the porous condition in silico.

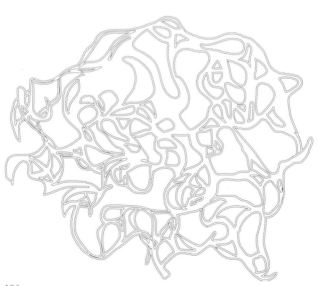

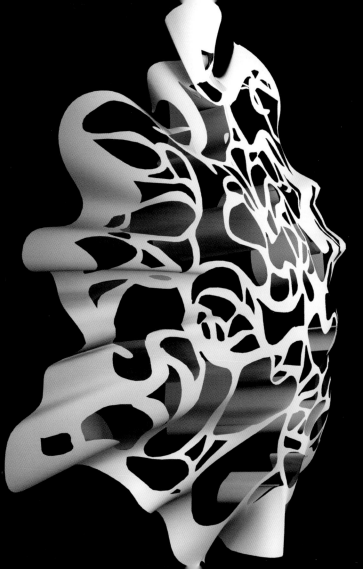

units

↓

cluster —————————————

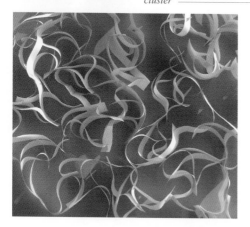

flow pattern along surface ◄—————————————

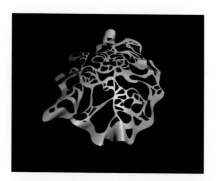

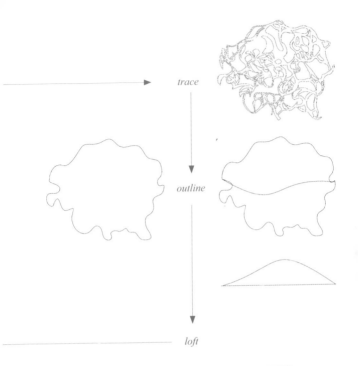

trace

outline

loft

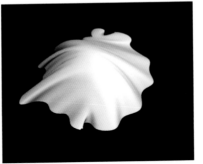

199

Pattern generation initiates with a digital image fragment of a regular 'meanderplex' cluster. A vector drawing of the fragment becomes the component of a regular two-dimensional aggregate. A diversified version is produced by combinations of variable enlargements of the elemental component. The pattern is cut and then wrapped, forming a hollow cylinder. Elements of pattern splines evoke structural capacity. Prototypes are fabricated in carton and aluminium sheets.

unit

↓

cluster

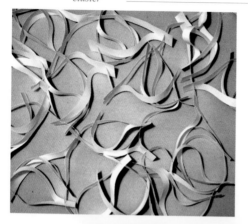

wrap ◄

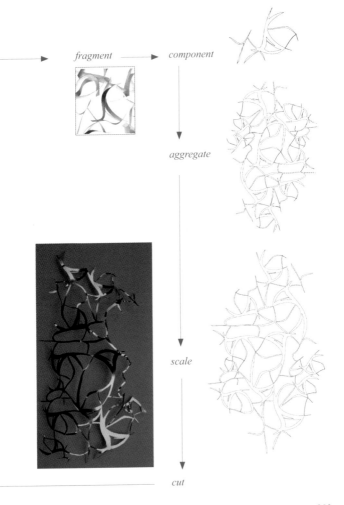

fragment → *component*

aggregate

scale

cut

pattern to furniture

Pattern generation initiates with a digital image fragment of a regular 'meanderplex' cluster. A vector drawing of the fragment is replicated into a series of rotations. The series is arrayed in rows. A curvilinear shape emerges in the overall pattern which is further streamlined, smoothed, and perforated through the surface. Folding the perforated surface into a possible seating position produces an elementary chair. The prototype is fabricated by laser cutter in carton.

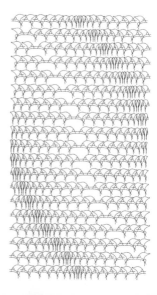

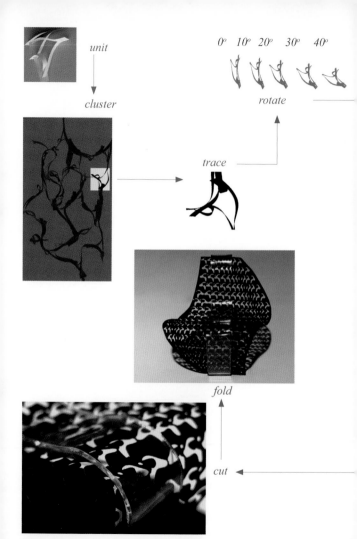

unit

cluster

0° 10° 20° 30° 40°

rotate

trace

fold

cut

206

numeric

array

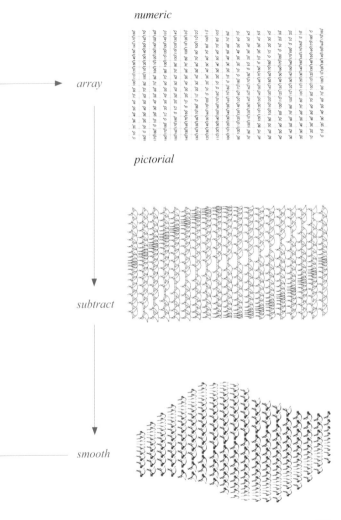

pictorial

subtract

smooth

The project investigates spherical geometry as a mathematic pro-
pedia of architectural curvilinearity. The assignment addressed
mathematical descriptions of Earth's only natural satellite, the
moon. Geometric interpretations of aerial views of the moon's
surface, its craters and seas were constructed by spherical triangles. Maintaining an equal radius of the circular arcs intersecting
the surface of the sphere, triangles with variable arc lengths were
constructed. Evaluating spherical triangle assembly options led
to the invention of an intricate geodesic pattern. The prototype
was fabricated in corrugated cardboard. Geodesic intricacy was
further modelled in Rhino.

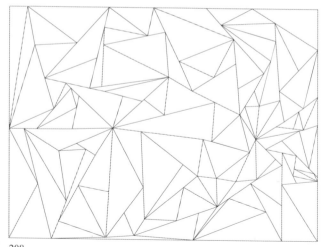

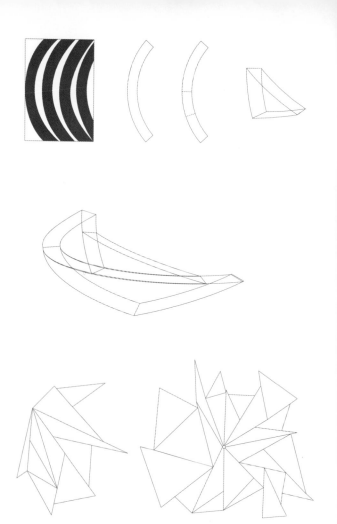

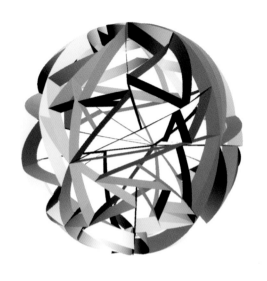

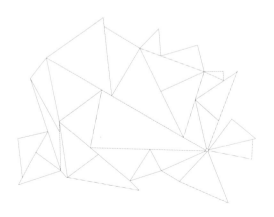

Colophon:

1.1 cut-stretch_
School of Design and Environment, National University of Singapore
Sophia Vyzoviti (faculty) and Neo Kae Young, 2006

1.2 'cut' hair salon
Matrix_g.sea/ Sophia Vyzoviti and Elina Karanastasi, 2007
Fabrication assistant: Constandia Manthou
Photography: Yiorgis Yerolymbos and Sophia Vyzoviti
Client : Vasilis Machairas
Location : Larissa, Greece
www.matrixgsea.blogspot.com

1.3 cut-enfold
Department of Architecture, University of Thessalyw
Sophia Vyzoviti (faculty) and Sophia Garnara, 2006

1.4 cut-pleat
Department of Architecture, University of Thessaly
Sophia Vyzoviti (faculty) and Theodor Grousopoulos, 2007

2.1 fishbones
Department of Architecture, University of Thessaly
Sophia Vyzoviti (faculty) and Helen Han, 2008

2.2 pleated shelter
Competition: Renewable energy sources and bioclimatic architecture for
shells to shelter people affected by natural disasters
Organization: Union International des Architectes (UiA) - Architecture
and Renewable Energy Sources (ARES)
Designers: Sophia Vyzoviti, Yota Adilenidou, Stergios Michos, 2007
Student Assistant: Valentina Karga
Consultancy: Myrto Chronaki, Stratos Manos, Elina Karanastasi

2.3 pleat and play
EASA007, city_index/ Supersurfaces Workshop
Tutors: Sophia Vyzoviti, Yota Adilenidou, Valentina Karga , 2007
Team: Ronan Kenny, Jernei Markelj, Nevenka Mancheva, Aleksandar
Petrovski, Ivana Mironska, Lana Barac, Monika Uszok, Ada Demetriu,
Tusienan Monica, Miro Craciun, Jordan Joanna
Location : Eleysina, Greece

2.4 pleat-revolve
EASA007, city_index/ Supersurfaces Workshop
Tutors: Sophia Vyzoviti, Yota Adilenidou, Valentina Karga, 2007
Department of Architecture, University of Thessaly
Sophia Vyzoviti (faculty) and Valentina Karga, 2007

2.5 pleat-tile
Department of Architecture, University of Thessaly
Sophia Vyzoviti (faculty) and Michael Christofi, 2008

3.1 folded brickwork
Competition: Housing and Shopping Complex in Metaxourgeion, Athens
Organization: GEK SA and DOMES Architectural Journal
Designers: Matrix_g.sea/ Sophia Vyzoviti, Elina Karanastasi and Yota
Adilenidou, 2006
Team: Vanghelis Dimitrakopoulos, Nikos Margaritis, Gregory Efstathia-
des, Constantine Galanopoulos
Consultuncy: Billy Gianutsu, Myrto Chronaki

3.2 mobius chain
EASA007, city_index/ Supersurfaces Workshop
Tutors: Sophia Vyzoviti, Yota Adilenidou, Valentina Karga , 2007
Team: Ronan Kenny, Jernei Markelj, Nevenka Mancheva, Aleksandar
Petrovski, Ivana Mironska, Lana Barac, Monika Uszok, Ada Demetriu,
Tusienan Monica, Miro Craciun, Jordan Joanna
Location : Eleysina, Greece

3.3 collapsible polygons
Department of Architecture, University of Thessaly
Sophia Vyzoviti (faculty) and Natasa Tarasi, 2007

3.4 rhomboids
Sophia Vyzoviti, 2008
Client : Papasotiriou Publishers
Location : Athens, Greece

3.5 grid formations
Department of Architecture, University of Thessaly
Sophia Vyzoviti (faculty) and Vlahou Antonia, 2007

3.6 textiles
Department of Architecture, University of Thessaly
Sophia Vyzoviti (faculty) Evi Brazioti, Maria Spastri, Katerina Tselebani, 2008

4.1 meanderplex
Department of Architecture, University of Thessaly
Sophia Vyzoviti (faculty), 2009
Team: Brenda Maria, Christos Anastasiou, Vaso Bogri, Dimitra Chatzi-
andreou, Mary Dimitriou, Natalia Douroundaki, Gregory Gregoriadis,
Archondi Ioannou, Maria Kallikouni, Panyotis Kaparaliotis, Panayotis
Karakitsos, Ioanna Karameri, Maria – Aliki Kostopoulou, Stelios Melini-
otis, Eytichia Stamataki, Fotis Rovolis, Konstantinos Stergiopoulos, Ileana
Toli, Anjia Zahariadou, Evi Zouzoula
Exhibition: The Archive_ Episode 3
Organization: Carteco Design Center
Curators: K&K architecs
www.thearchive.gr

4.1.1 pattern to relief
Department of Architecture, University of Thessaly
Sophia Vyzoviti (faculty), Anja Zahariadou, Konstantinos Stergiopoulos,
2009

4.1.2 pattern to facet
Department of Architecture, University of Thessaly
Sophia Vyzoviti (faculty), Natalia Douroundaki, Panayotis Kaparaliotis,
2009

4.1.3 pattern to surface
Department of Architecture, University of Thessaly

Sophia Vyzoviti (faculty), Archondi Ioannou, 2009

4.1.4 pattern to structure

Department of Architecture, University of Thessaly
Sophia Vyzoviti (faculty), Vaso Bogri, 2009

4.1.5 pattern to furniture

Department of Architecture, University of Thessaly
Sophia Vyzoviti (faculty), Gregory Gregoriadis, Maria Kallikouni, 2009

4.2 parametric moon

Department of Architecture, University of Thessaly
Sophia Vyzoviti (faculty), Nikolaos Georgakas, 2010
Team: Myrsini Chalayti, Maria Flessa, Isavella Karouti, Panyotis Kaparaliotis, Panayotis Karakitsos, Iro Mazaraki, Fotis Rovolis, Michalis Thanos , Ileana Toli, Anjia Zahariadou, Evi Zouzoula
www.supersurfaces-supersurfaces.blogspot.com